IMAGES
of America
SHREWSBURY
VOLUME II

This tiny post office on the island that separates the Sycamore Avenue traffic lanes, east of Broad Street, is perhaps the most curious and fascinating structure ever erected in Shrewsbury. Seen here in a 1940s photograph, it was built by Harry G. Borden in 1924, and two years later it was leased by the post office. In 1956, the post office moved to its present location in the Shrewsbury Shops (p.24). The borough later occupied this building for use as a borough hall and police headquarters. The small, obsolete, and difficult-to-adapt structure was demolished in May 1966. (The Dorn's Collection.)

IMAGES
of America

SHREWSBURY
VOLUME II

Randall Gabrielan

ARCADIA
PUBLISHING

Published by Arcadia Publishing
Charleston, South Carolina

Library of Congress Catalog Card Number: 97-134552

For all general information contact Arcadia Publishing at:
Telephone 843-853-2070
Fax 843-853-0044
E-mail sales@arcadiapublishing.com
For customer service and orders:
Toll-Free 1-888-313-2665

Visit us on the Internet at www.arcadiapublishing.com

This book is dedicated to Kathy Dorn Severini, a native of Shrewsbury, who still revels in the qualities that made the town a special place to grow up. A trained singer and skilled photographer, she embodies the Dorn family qualities of cheerfulness, optimism, and friendliness. As manager of the classic photo operations at Photography Unlimited by Dorn's, she often works with the historical community. Kathy is a careful organizer and conscientious curator of a collection that has enhanced many Images of America titles. Her invaluable work makes her as vital a part of the pictorial preservation process as the author or the publisher. Thanks for being you, Kathy.

CONTENTS

Acknowledgments   6

Introduction   7

1.   Broad Street   9

2.   Sycamore Avenue   47

3.   The Four Corners   69

4.   Schools   93

5.   People, Places, and Events   101

ACKNOWLEDGMENTS

This book could not have been done without the help of many generous people who lent photographs for this project. My thanks and gratitude to all.

The depth of coverage in the collection of Photography Unlimited by Dorn's is growing for numerous towns around their Red Bank base. Their Shrewsbury holdings are particularly rich and have contributed a significant number of images to this volume, which enhance the book's theme of the making of a modern town.

Virginia Herden Mohan has a deep love and affection for her native town and a collection that shows well both family and their surroundings. Her pictures were shared with enthusiasm and support meriting special mention.

John Rhody, Monmouth County's most enthusiastic postcard collector and my longtime supporter, offered stunning photographic postcards of a town not well traveled by postcard publishers.

The staunch support of the Shrewsbury Historical Society, and Francis and Margaret Borden included loans for the first volume that also produced several images for this one.

Elizabeth Curley Wurst and John Curley, whose father James was in the vanguard of Shrewsbury's modern development, contributed several fine images, demonstrating that family photographs are often also historical documents.

Joseph Hammond, historian of Christ Church, who led a preservation effort that rescued one of the county's most important buildings from imminent danger, offered several fine images of the restoration project, demonstrating that history is on going everyday.

Thanks, too, to Olga Boeckel, Joseph Eid, Harriet Kodama, Scott Longfield and the Two River Times, Monroe Marx, Jeanne Van Dorn Mauk, the Monmouth County Historical Association, Anna Morford, Donna Patterson, Robert Pelligrini, Anna Louise Campbell Rudner, Robert Schoeffling, Joann and Thomas Smith, and Al Tomaino.

And last, but not least, thanks to my wife Barbara Ann Gabrielan for lending me her camera for several of the contemporary photographs.

INTRODUCTION

"The Making of a Modern Town"

Two perspectives can be taken on Shrewsbury's history. The longer view sees one of New Jersey's earliest settlements, c. 1665, dating from the beginning of the Europeans' arrival in Monmouth County. The shorter view focuses on a 20th-century municipality, formed in 1926. The Borough of Shrewsbury assumed its current character in the post-World War II years and has since undergone significant changes that continue into the present. This volume focuses on the latter perspective.

The village of Shrewsbury in its early years, the term used in the informal sense of a small settlement, was the core of a vast area that embraced much of Monmouth County and all of Ocean County. The core of that settlement remains in the borough, the heir of Shrewsbury's 17th-century origins, which remains separated from its corporate existence.

Shrewsbury Township had been dismembered over many decades. After it lost Little Silver in 1923 through that borough's incorporation, Shrewsbury Township was left an area embracing today's Tinton Falls, Shrewsbury Borough and the one-tenth of a square mile that became Vail Homes shortly before World War II. Vail Homes is all that remains today of the Township. Development of the surroundings of the village's quiet, "exclusive" rural pocket was getting uncomfortably close in southern Red Bank and areas just beyond the Red Bank border. The small houses on tiny lots did not suit Sycamore Avenue's idea of local exclusivity.

The borough's zoning law was passed four years after the 1926 incorporation. Two streets were reserved for business: Newman Springs Road, on the Red Bank border, and the part of Broad Street (Highway 35) south of the railroad to Sycamore Avenue. Broad Street retained its residential character for over 25 years, and maintained a wide ratio of residences to businesses into the 1960s. Broad Street was still pedestrian-friendly until the widening of the roadway c. 1961.

Larger buildings were not erected until the 1970s, which brought the Red Cross Building (1971), mitigated by sitting back from the road, and the Shrewsbury State Bank (1974), which was located at the commercialized northern end. However, they fit without overwhelming the landscape, perhaps because all available space had not been filled and the buildings were relatively modest.

The announcement of plans for The Grove brought local dismay and the expression of wishes that the land, prime undeveloped acreage in a commercial zone, could remain vacant. Completion of the project brought Shrewsbury an attractive ratable development without the feared congestion. The recent promotion of The Grove in conjunction with Red Bank expresses the realization that Broad Street is now a single, automotive-age thoroughfare that transcends municipal borders.

Southern Broad Street's growth began with a public building, the Monmouth County Eastern Branch Library, and continued near the borders with shopping strips, a newspaper plant (now offices), and office buildings. One remaining undeveloped tract makes it apparent that the end of growth may be nearing. However, it may be a replacement structure that best illustrates how growth affects the landscape. The demolition of the former Williamsburg office, proportioned like a house, with larger structures (p.36–37) suggests that maximum land use rather than the former mix of commercial and residential occupancies will prevail on Broad Street.

Curley homes also helped transform the borough. The subdivision of estates began in the 1930s, but early examples, such as Buttonwood Park and Silverbrook maintained the town's character with individual, distinctive structures. A large number of its early residents were servicemen returning from WW II. It may be said that they helped democratize the exclusive borough after liberating the overrun nations.

Growth in Shrewsbury has been accomplished while leaving intact most of its historic character. That process often requires considerable private commitment, as with Christ Church, pps.72–76, or public resolve, as in the campaign to preserve the Borough Hall. The book was planned and written during that apparently successful struggle, one that should keep both readers and the author ever-mindful that modernity should not sacrifice historic integrity.

Errata: Volume I

p.18 top John Boyd was ordained by the first Presbytery in this country, not county.
p.23 top Tinker Dorn was a member of the Red Bank High School class of 1964.
p.58 top Demolition of 795 Broad Street occurred in May 1959.
p.81 top Charles Francis Borden died December 19, 1960, not 1920.
p.91 top Mrs. Hazard appears to be at the left of the groom.
p.117 top The pictured school was on Broad Street.

One

BROAD STREET

The May 9, 1959 parade on Broad Street celebrated the 50th anniversary of the Shrewsbury Hose Company and dedicated a new recreation field (p.122). Many organizations participated, including the Girl Scouts, led by Barbara Cavanaugh, left, and Kathy Dorn Severini. The west side of Broad has changed; plain stucco now covers the two-story stores on the corner of Obre Place, and one-story stores replaced the adjacent gas station. (The Dorn's Collection.)

Fioretti's Farm market stood on the northernmost stem of the east side of Broad Street. The family is remembered fondly as nice people, selling fine produce and readily accepting the customer's word in case of a questionable product. It was torn down by Al Tomaino in 1953, the date of this image, to be replaced by the gas station seen on the top of p.14. (Al Tomaino.)

The side of Fioretti's and the part of the front of the house south of it, shown at top, are pictured here, also in 1953. The house, once occupied by Police Chief Otto Herden and later as a barracks for state police troops, was demolished in 1961 for the erection of four stores. (Al Tomaino.)

Ann Fioretti Hayes, left, and Eleanor Jenkins Swannell, take a break at the Fioretti stand in the early 1950s.

451 Broad is seen here in the late 1950s before the construction of the gas station seen on p. 14. (Al Tomaino.)

The hamburger stand that once occupied the southwest corner of Broad and Newman Springs Road is seen in a c.1930s photograph. The smiling waitress is unidentified, but helps us see an early glimpse of the highway at a time when a local burger place could get away with a simple, though uninspired claim of featuring "those tasty morsels."

The house with two partial glimpses on p. 10 is seen here on its south elevation in the early 1940s with family members of the resident. William Herden, son of the chief, is the adult, while the children are, from left: Virginia Herden, her cousin Brendan Sheedy, James Devaney, Emily Smith, and Norman Smith.

A generous garden filled the lot between the house at top and the hosiery mill to the south. The latter building is now the hardware store and bank offices at 457 Broad. In the garden in this early 1940s photograph, from left to right are: Emmy Smith, Bill Herden, Norman Smith, Virginia Herden, Jim Devaney, and Brendan Sheedy.

James Herden and his calf depict the rural character of the land behind Broad in 1937.

This 1960 photograph, showing Broad Street prior to the construction of the jug-handle turn lane for Newman Springs Road, places the Shrewsbury Diner (Vol. I, p.105) in its street context, seen under the sign in the rear. Al Tomaino built the gas station in 1953. (The Dorn's Collection.)

The construction of the jug-handle lane, seen here in December 1962, required the removal of the diner, which after many years on the west side of Broad Street at Shrewsbury Avenue, was replaced in 1997 by the larger American Diner. The new diner also took a piece of the service station's property, making that occupancy no longer viable and resulting in the construction of new stores still on the site. Note the former hosiery mill at right, now the hardware store and bank office at 457 Broad. (The Dorn's Collection.)

14

Pictured here are the railroad tracks form Shrewsbury's northeast border with Red Bank. At left rear is Maple Avenue, which the state highway department designated as part of Highway 35, in order to reduce Broad Street, Red Bank traffic. Maple merges into Broad Street, Shrewsbury, which is also part of Highway 35. "Jug-handle" is New Jersey road terminology; the aerial on the bottom of the opposite page eases comprehension of the term. (The Dorn's Collection.)

Halloween was a festive occasion at Buxton's Restaurant, shown in this photograph c.1970s. At least one employee was having a devil of a time and even the landlord got into the act. That's "Dr." Al Tomaino, second from right. This was a rare instance when Yosemite Sam's body language did not say "back off." Buxton was remodeled into the pizza place that opened in 1982. (Al Tomaino.)

Alf Zomo's Midway Motor Service at 450 Broad Street looks like, well, a garage, and a not particularly appealing one in this *c.*1950s photograph. (The Dorn's Collection.)

A few modifications by Shrewsbury architect Gerard A. Barba gave this facade an attractive Colonial Revival appearance. The remodeling and the extension on the southern side were built *c.* 1961. Monmouth Stereo now occupies the premises. (The Dorn's Collection.)

Sherman's was a Red Bank decorator whose workroom was on the west side of Shrewsbury's Broad Street, across from White Road. Their fleet is seen here in a 1961 photograph. (The Dorn's Collection.)

Union Laundry at the southwest corner of Monroe Avenue, seen in the 1950s, sent its dry-cleaning to Newark. Perhaps the volume of a larger facility permitted the proffered savings. Royal Tire is in the building now. (The Dorn's Collection.)

17

The Shrewsbury Dairy, organized in 1919, succeeded the Albert Grover dairy. Since the 1920s it had occupied this building erected by the Shrewsbury Improvement Company at the northeast corner of Broad and White Road. This photograph from the White Road side dates *c.* mid-1950s. The buildings were demolished *c.* 1970, and the bank seen opposite now occupies the site. (The Dorn's Collection.)

An unidentified Shrewsbury Dairy delivery man is seen on his rounds in a Divco truck in Red Bank, December 1956. (The Dorn's Collection.)

Built in the 1970s, the headquarters of the Shrewsbury State Bank, on the former Shrewsbury Dairy site, is a handsome Colonial Revival design that reflects the origins of its home where it was founded to provide "hometown banking." The bank has established a local branch network over the years, including some in retail stores. The large financial institutions across the Hudson might realize there is an enormous customer base outside the shadows of their towers that values a bank in a supermarket more than a supermarket of financial services.

Arnone's Texaco station at the southeast corner of 473 Broad Street and White Road, is a reminder of a time when oil industry profit orientation was directed to the retail operation, resulting in many smaller stations, often in close proximity. This station was rebuilt to face White Road and is now an auto lubrication business. (The Dorn's Collection.)

The 1959, pre-road widening photograph of the northern stem of Broad Street, looking north from Monroe Avenue, makes it easy to comprehend why the space between stores and pavement is so narrow today. The Puritan Dairy at right, long the home of Hilo Steiner's lighting shop until its December 1996 closing, is now a clothing retailer. The former Singing Wheels skating rink at left, previously the Smoke Shop Tavern, is now the clothing store Annie Sez. (The Dorn's Collection.)

The Davis Marx family's party, c. 1960s, provides a good glimpse of the interior of the Singing Wheels rink. Mrs. Marx is the adult in the back, toward the left, while Marlene Marx is the girl in front in the dark jumper. David Stillman gazes upward towards the left in the second row. The short girl in front, with her outfit identical to Marlene's, but partially covered by a coat, is a second Marx daughter. Sam Phillips is the boy in the back row at left. (The Dorn's Collection.)

The contestants and the name of the 1949 beauty contest at Singing Wheels are unknown. Their smiles are pleasant, but their bathing suits are dull beyond reason. See p.113 to compare them with the more stylish suits a quarter century later. (The Dorn's Collection.)

The first three finishers are unidentified, but their ranks can be inferred from the size of their trophies. (The Dorn's Collection.)

The remaining team members are unidentified, with the exception of no. 46, Joe Dean, who signed the back of this photographic postcard. The winners are not known, but the author would have backed the woman at left, in the back row, if her legs were as sturdy as her right arm. (Glenn Vogel.)

Singing Wheels was the site of marathon dancing around 1933. A group of unidentified dancers are seen here in an undated photograph from that period.

Many of the marathon dancers had the same style publicity photographs printed on postcard stock. Mary Herden (p.125) collected them, with the inscription in the lower left reflecting a fond tie between participants and viewers.

This 1960 aerial shows a developing Broad Street, with the Shrewsbury Shops at left. Other retailers would fill the adjacent space, including a supermarket at one time. A soft ice cream stand, a rug shop, the laundry (p.17), and Singing Wheels fill the row. The latter, then half the building's present size, still had the Alexander Denis house behind it. (The Dorn's Collection.)

A closer look at the Shrewsbury Shops in 1960 caused present owner Al Tomaino to remark, "Look at the cars parked any old way. I'd never stand for that." The Grove filled the field on the east side of Broad. (The Dorn's Collection.)

24

This 1959 aerial looking east includes Marx Brothers land that the firm wished to use for expansion of its slaughterhouse operation. Residents of Buttonwood Park, a cluster of quality homes north of Sycamore Avenue, were among the opponents of a needed variance, resulting in construction of a new abattoir on the west side of Broad. Visible next to the unsightly intrusion of billboards are the old firehouse and Library Hall. (The Dorn's Collection.)

Two older houses in the foreground are the backdrop of extensive construction west of Broad in this 1953 aerial. The McCue house (p. 36) is at bottom, while the home (both in 1953 and today) of Monroe and Effie Marx is adjacent, in front of that year's major expansion of the Shrewsbury Borough School. Shadow Brook is north of this scene. New houses on Queen Anne Drive, cut through the Shadow Brook estate, are pictured at top. (The Dorn's Collection.)

The building at left provided instant recognition of the spot and elevation of the photographer of this unidentified photo postcard postmarked Shrewsbury April 26, 1909. The photograph was taken from the top of the newly completed Shrewsbury Borough School, looking at the George Washington Stillwell house that would become the superintendent's residence at Shadow Brook. The hills of Red Bank are in the right background, while one of the houses in the right foreground stands adjacent to the present Grove shopping center, built in the former Shadow Brook field behind the house. (John Rhody.)

Remodeling the house at top was an early step in Dr. Ernest Fahnestock's building of a country residence and farm group. Ray Stillman, the real estate developer who, in 1942, bought and subdivided the Fahnestock estate, occupied it back then. It has lacked residential occupancy for years and has been vacant in the recent past, though there have been recent reports of a possible 1998 sale to another commercial occupant. (The Dorn's Collection.)

The companion to the photograph opposite shows the east side of Broad, just south of White Street, but includes houses on that side street on a diagonal. Number 697 at right now houses a medical office. A c. 1915 house fills the vacant lot, while no. 685, adjacent on the left, still looks like this 1909 photograph, as does the house at far left. (John Rhody.)

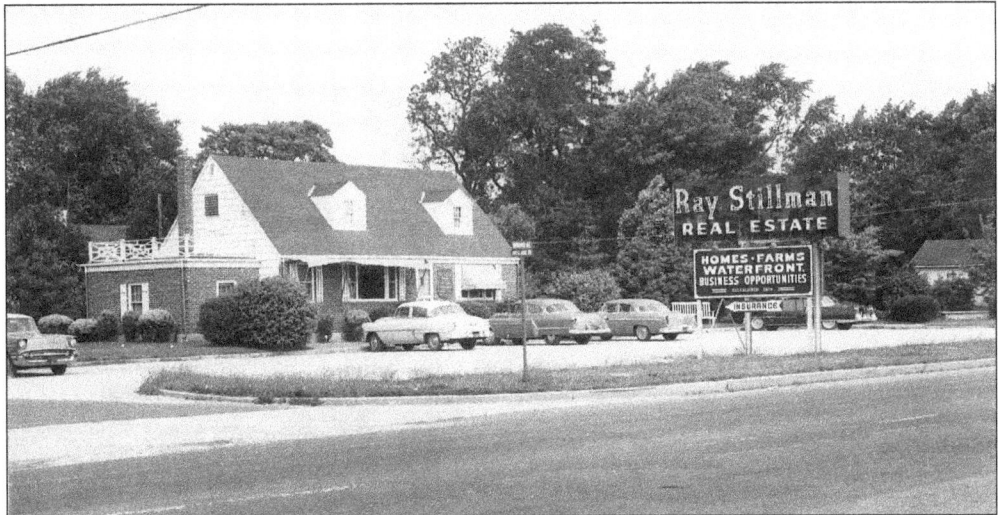

Raymond H. Stillman, after buying the Fahnestock estate for a reported $25,000, occupied its former George Washington Stillwell house as his residence. He built this new real estate office south of his home, at 648 Broad Street, in the late 1940s. Today, it is still a real estate office, occupied by Brokers & Realtors. This photograph is c.1955. (The Dorn's Collection.)

This 1950s photograph from Queen Anne Drive looking north embraces many of the houses built on Shadowbrook property and the estate's farm group, which is the line of buildings parallel with Broad Street bisecting the photograph. The Grove shops were built on the large field, closing the last major open space in the business district. The cluster of buildings on the first several pages of this chapter are along Broad's northern stem. The diagonal at top is the railroad. (The Dorn's Collection.)

The Hearth was a popular roadside eatery, built around a large, well, hearth. It is seen here at 600 Broad Street in 1958. The Hearth was remodeled into Gloria Nilson's real estate office in 1977, the year she purchased the property. (The Dorn's Collection.)

28

Gloria Nilson grew up on Staten Island, moved to a Colts Neckfarm, her father's retirement haven, in her teens, and later graduated from Goucher College with a degree in psychology. She entered the real estate business in 1961 with Walker and Walker, where she maintained a consistent record as their top sales agent. Gloria founded Gloria Nilson Realtors in 1977, two years before this photograph was taken.

The Hearth was incorporated into Gloria Nilson's Logo, barely visible in the sign. The exterior changes were so slight that Hearth customers, conversing rather than looking around in the parking lot, were heard exclaiming on entering, "What, no burgers?"

Architect Gerard A. Barba's office at 673 Broad Street, a typical vernacular house from the turn of the century, was likely built by a carpenter from stock plans. The photograph is c. 1960 of a building appearing to have been unchanged for decades. (The Dorn's Collection.)

Several decorative enhancements and the reconstruction of the porch beautified the building, as well as making it functional for his architecture practice. Care has maintained the appearance seen in this 1961 photograph, taken shortly after completion. (The Dorn's Collection.)

Broad Street is seen looking north from Obre Place in 1939, a time when it had more trees and fewer businesses.

The back of the Pierce farm on the west side of Broad Street is the background for this c. mid-1930s photograph of Molly McDonald and her daughter Mary, the grandmother and mother of the lender, Virginia Herden Mohan.

This photograph of an August 1936 accident provides a glimpse of the east side of Broad Street near the stream and north of the present site of The Grove. The near field appears planted in corn. Lovett later owned a piece of this ground (Vol. I, p.44), once part of Fahnestock's Shadow Brook estate.

This photograph is a companion to the one opposite at bottom. Familiarity with the background houses may help pinpoint the exact spot of the accident.

A schism developed among members of the Religious Society of Friends. The Hixites, liberal followers of Elias Hicks, retained the original meetinghouse site, while the "old" orthodox members moved to a Broad Street house. The building was named Library Hall at the time of this 1896 photograph.

NATHAN MARX   MARTIN MARX

Shrewsbury, N. J., // / 191 3

M~ Emmon

BOUGHT OF

MARX BROS.

Dealers in and Shippers of

LIVE CATTLE, SHEEP,

Lambs, Calves, Hogs, Etc.

Telephone 296 Red Bank.   TERMS CASH

Some early 20th-century dining practices can be inferred from this Marx Bros. bill, part of an $8.31 tab for one month's delivery of seven items. Liver was 12¢ per pound. One is getting old if he remembers when this cholesterol-laden organ was regarded as a health food. Ham was 20¢, but the author dined on 59¢-per-pound ham the day he acquired the billhead, though it admittedly was a big off-season sale, but far cheaper in 1998 dollars. Two steaks and an unspecified roast had no details other than the sums billed.

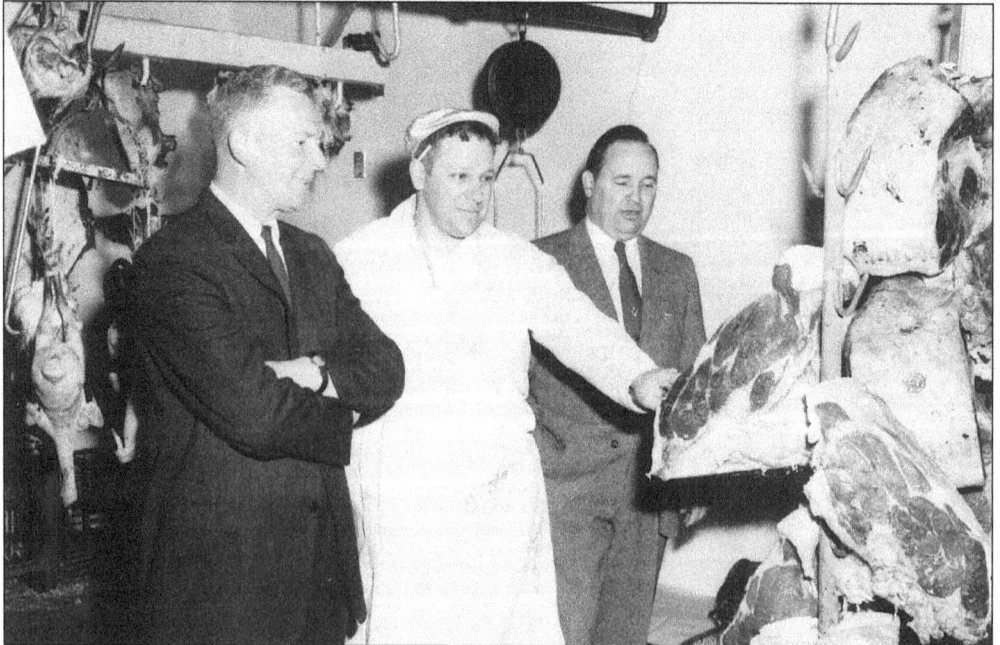

Monroe Marx, center, is showing the meat he would be cutting for the Presbyterian Men's Club steak roast in May 1958. Charles Mahan accompanies the event's chairman Rodney Barnes at left. The meat is hips of beef for sirloin steaks. Note the chickens at left, sold with their feet at the customer's request. (The Dorn's Collection.)

34

Mrs. Bud Johnson's appealing pose, made in July 1943, also provides a glimpse of Broad Street looking north, from north of the firehouse.

Monroe Marx is seen receiving the Businessman of the Year Award in 1978, being pinned by Suzanne Ruoff, vice president of the Shrewsbury Business and Professional Association. Monroe's public service embraces a long list, many with lengthy tenure and leadership positions, including the Shrewsbury Board of Education, the Board of Health, the juvenile court, Shrewsbury Hose Company, the Planning Board, and the Special Police.

Vincent McCue Sr., whose family had owned 746 Broad Street since 1913, sold the property to a developer in December 1977. The Second Empire-style house (Vol. I, p.53) was destroyed by fire on February 7, 1978. It had been feared that someone was sleeping in the vacant house, but the place was found empty. Broad Street would be a little less residential after the sale.

The Williamsburg Associates office, which some regarded as a commercial intrusion, was a modest structure that fit well in the Broad Street environment. Built on the McCue lot, it looked like a house and reflected the traditional styles often utilized by the firm, which built several fine developments in the area. The building stood for fewer than 20 years. Vacant in the mid-1990s, it was demolished in 1996 and replaced by a larger building (top, opposite).

The size of Vincent Russo's office at 748 Broad Street, completed in 1997, dwarfs the former Williamsburg building at bottom opposite. However, it does not use all of the plot's permitted space, but reinforces the business utility of northern Broad. The design, of Virginia colonial inspiration, is stylistically consistent with the 18 Russo offices and originated with the owner, Vincent J. Russo, and his son, V.J. Russo III, known as Jimmy.

The Monroe and Effie Marx home at 720 Broad Street, with c. 1850 origins, was one of few structures on the Red Bank-Eatontown Highway during its early decades. The change of Broad Street's character now makes it appear lost among the large surrounding brick offices and school. The house was purchased by his grandfather Frank in 1906. After a period of ownership outside the family, Monroe acquired it in 1946.

The Shrewsbury Hose Company was posed in front of their truck in 1939. Monroe Marx lent the picture and recalled his associates, including Robert Yorg, standing at left. From left to right they are: (kneeling) Jim Poole, Chet Ferrar, Everett Anderson, and Emerson Pierce; (standing) two unidentified members, Al Robertson, Frank Lane, Fred Yorg, Moose Herden, and John Poole (John Parker is seated in the truck.); (seated at top) unidentified, Chief Ed Honahan, Fritz Yorg, Sam Yorg, and Monroe Marx.

The firemen of the Shrewsbury Hose Company in this July 1939 photograph include Bill Herden and Alonzo Devaney (sixth and seventh from the right of the truck), father and uncle of the lender, Virginia Herden Mohan, and Francis Sagurton at the extreme right.

These three buildings on a familiar stem of the east side of Broad, seen in a 1956 photograph, are gone. A new firehouse was built north of this one c. 1962. Library Hall, the site of theatricals (Vol. I, p.45), a variety of social activities, and in its later years, storage for Marx Bros., was demolished around then. Close inspection of the aerial on the top of p.25 reveals the former Frank and Fannie Marx house, left, at 795 Broad, to be in the process of demolition in May, 1959. A store is on the site now. (The Dorn's Collection.)

Enjoying themselves at an unidentified event at the Shrewsbury firehouse, c. early 1950s, are from left to right as follows: (front row) Frederick Yorg, his wife Verna, and Eleanor Yorg and her husband Sam; (back row) Mrs. and Mr. Joseph Hopko, an unidentified woman, her escort David Emmons, Emily Curley, and James A. Curley.

The bell, donated by the First Presbyterian Church of Red Bank and mounted on a tower paid for by Dr. Ernest Fahnestock, was removed from the old firehouse in August 1962, prior to its demolition. The bell is now mounted on the ground in front of the present firehouse. (The Dorn's Collection.)

William W. Gibson, right, newly elected chief of the Shrewsbury Hose Company, receives the white chief's helmet from Albert Hancher, left, ex-chief and then first assistant engineer, and Samuel Johnson, first assistant chief, in a December 1974 photograph. The mosaic mural in the background was made by the Shrewsbury Borough School art students of Lois E. Eben.

Old timers' night at Shrewsbury Hose Company on June 27, 1976 was the occasion for honoring their long-serving members. From left to right are as follows: David Emmons, George Reynolds, and Frank Lane, who had served 45, 58, and 45 years respectively.

Mayor Dorothy B. Manson is about to christen the Shrewsbury Hose Company No. 1's new Hahn pumper at a June 1978 dedication. Also present, from left to right were: Sam Johnson, (chairman of the truck committee); Councilman Robert D. Standley (chairman of the fire committee); Chief James D. Martin, and Second Assistant Chief William Gibson.

The relocation of the Red Bank Register to Broad Street Shrewsbury in 1973 marked a major expansion of their facility. Management searched the country for design inspiration. Shrewsbury architect Gerard A. Barba modeled this building after a Columbus Indiana building.

The Register's new press is seen in 1978, one with color capability. Other technological change came in that decade, including typesetting by computer.

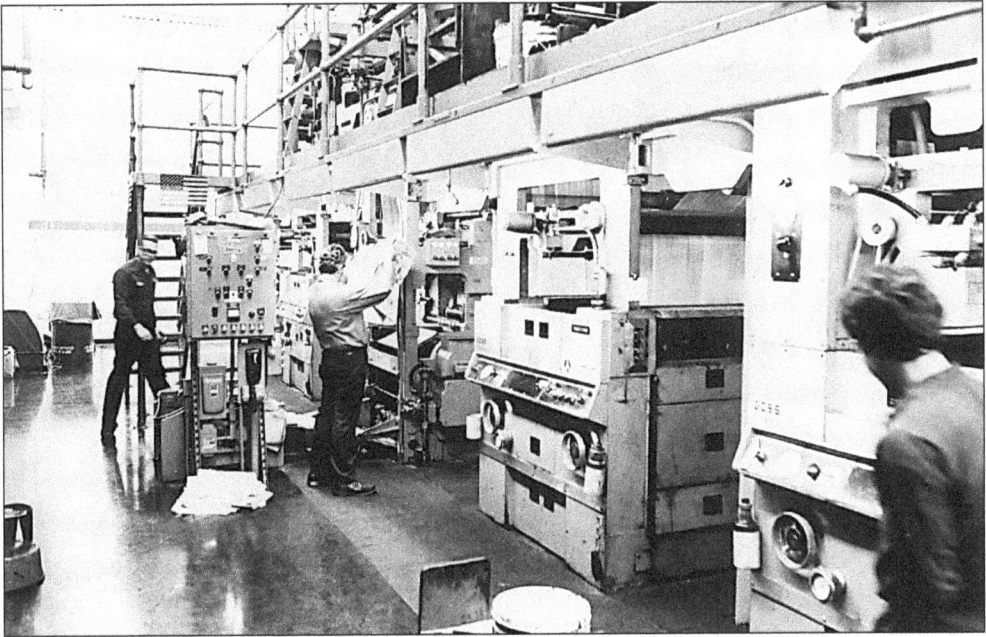

The Register building had large windows, making the press visible to a passing public. Although the Shrewsbury location was not conducive to that arrangement, a spacious layout was made to permit visitors during working hours, a tour the author remembers fondly.

Eight young paper deliverers were gathered outside the Register building in 1975 with their newly issued red delivery bags. They are from left to right as follows: (kneeling) John Degnan, Sekhar Ranaswamy, Jeff Rowse, and Patty Weiler; (standing) Hugh Kearney, Leo Kirohwar, Chris O'Connor, and Raymon Dlug. The great American tradition for instilling a youthful work ethic and thrift, through the delivery of afternoon papers after school, is lost locally, as the area's last daily now publishes in the morning and insists on adult carriers.

Broad Street looking south from Silverbrook Road was a pastoral scene in 1939. The Straus estate was beyond on the left (east) and the polo field on the right.

This 1953 aerial shows Shrewsbury's southern tip. Shrewsbury Avenue, in front, merges with Broad Street, the triangle now the site of the Shrewsbury Plaza shopping center. The parking lot below it is in Tinton Falls. The Straus estate on the east side of Broad now includes the library (opposite) and a strip center. Fort Monmouth buildings are visible at right, and the meandering course of Parkers Creek, Shrewsbury's border, is discernible north of them. (The Dorn's Collection.)

44

The Brookside Inn on the east side of Broad was a period roadhouse. The building, standing across from the diner at the juncture of Shrewsbury Avenue, is easy to overlook at the entrance to the busy jug-handle turning lane. Virginia is standing in front of her parents, Mary and Bill Herden, on Easter Day, 1947.

The original outlines of the Monmouth County Eastern Branch Library are seen from the air in this 1969 photograph. It was designed by Howell Lewis Shay, F.A.I.A., and built in 1968 by Henry V. Vaccaro Construction Co. An extension on the south and east was erected in 1991. (The Dorn's Collection.)

The former home and private school of Theodosia Finch at 830 Broad was remodeled as a Red Cross headquarters in 1944 and purchased by them the following year. The offices eventually became inadequate and were demolished in 1971. This photograph is c. 1950, when a sign was needed to encourage parking off the street. (The Dorn's Collection.)

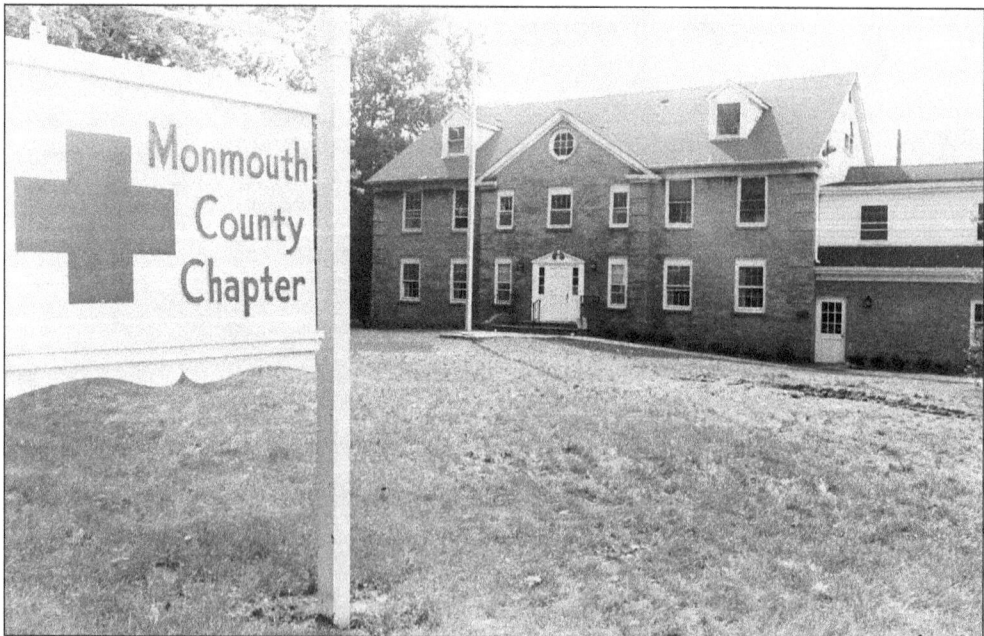

The Monmouth County Chapter of the American Red Cross, later renamed the Jersey Shore Chapter, built this colonial-inspired office in the rear of the house at top in 1971. The structure incurred fire damage shortly after opening, but was soon repaired. This photograph is dated September 1971.

Two

SYCAMORE AVENUE

The Fred Van Dorn marriage to Elizabeth Hope Johnson in 1905 at the Presbyterian Church was the occasion for this striking horse and carriage photograph. It was taken in front of the 1890 Benjamin White house at 355 Sycamore Avenue. The well-preserved house, seen in its street context on p.102 of Vol. I, was later prominent as Fordacre, the home of George Ford Morris, the noted painter of animals. Art has recently returned to the house, now the studio and "Art In the Barn" classroom for fine artist Robyn Ellenbogen.

Randolph Borden expanded the house at 345 Sycamore Avenue in the 1890s, a structure attributed to *c.* 1790. This December 1932 photograph long postdates the *c.* 1900 picture on p. 80 of Vol. I, but the snow and mature plantings preclude a detailed examination of differences.

A tennis club was an active component of the Shrewsbury social-sporting scene from the 1890s. This photograph, perhaps from that period, is believed to be the Randolph Borden courts; the unidentified crew may include some Bordens.

The Presbyterian manse, the former Stewert Van Vliet house at 348 Sycamore Avenue, is depicted during an unidentified July 1953 event. The church bought the house in 1952. It was initially used as a Sunday school building. Lois Joice, the minister's wife and Shrewsbury's first female councilwoman, is seen here between two unidentified women. (The Dorn's Collection.)

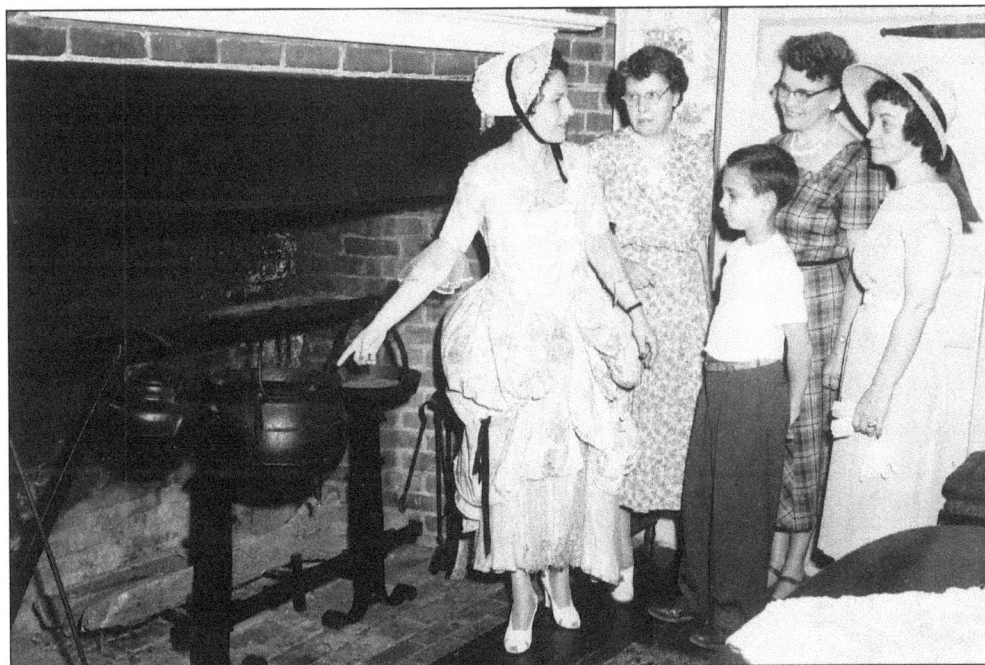

The charming woman at left in the photograph at top is now inside making a point about a fireplace, presumably in the same house. To her left is Miss Huelsen, a longtime resident of the Allen house; the others are unidentified. (The Dorn's Collection.)

This c. 1905 postcard view south from 291 Sycamore Avenue depicts a quiet, tree-lined street with buildings set back from the road. One, beyond view in the background, would have been Hazard's ketchup factory. Today a commercial occupant on Sycamore Avenue is unthinkable. Over-sentimentalizers of the so-called good old days (they were awful) should remember that there was no land-use control then. (John Rhody.)

The Assembly of God, seen in a 1958 photograph, is the newest house of worship on historic Sycamore Avenue. (The Dorn's Collection.)

Irving J. Feist, president of the Newark real estate firm Feist & Feist, resided at 300 Sycamore Avenue in the Dr. Paul Livingston house completed in 1928 (Vol. I, p.96). Feist, raised in Newark, joined the firm his father founded in 1904, following graduation from the University of Pennsylvania's Wharton School. He served on many industry and public bodies and was best known for his long-term service to the Boy Scouts of America. Seen here in a 1973 photograph, Feist died in 1978.

Anne D. Campbell, a 1970s resident of 300 Sycamore Avenue, was prominent in Democratic Party circles. She was vice-chairwoman of the New Jersey State Convention, held various national level positions, and was an executive officer of the 1982 Democratic National Convention in New York. Campbell, seen in her home in 1977, was a partner in a Washington public affairs and lobbying firm at her untimely death in 1995 at age 50.

"SHREWSBURY"

Tomato Ketchup

Will not Mould or Lose its Flavor.

Guaranteed to Keep in any Climate.

SHREWSBURY TOMATOKETCHUP is an article of standard excellence, with a flavor certain to please the palate of the most fastidious bon vivant, and which connoisseurs everywhere pronounce incomparably fine. Color, taste, aroma are faultless.

It is admirable with hot and cold meats, oyster stews, fish, and gives a superior flavor to gravies, deviled kidneys, or any delicate preparation of meat. With chops, veal cutlets, and baked beans it is simply delicious, and it is a great addition to macaroni or hot buttered toast.

We have used the SHREWSBURY TOMATOKETCHUP on our tables since its first introduction, to the extent of about two hundred dozen bottles per year, and regard it as the finest condiment of its kind ever brought to our notice.

W. D. GARRISON,
Manager Grand Union Hotel.

Manufactured and for Sale by

E. C. HAZARD & CO., NEW YORK.

Hazard's advertising underscored his brand to distinguish himself from competitors. This ad, appearing in the *Red Bank Register* in the 1890s, presumably was used elsewhere, but it does not describe his factory's locale as the origin of the name. The illustrated ad was informative, but humorous ads were also used.

Hazard bought the Broadmeadow tomato factory from Gordon Sickles in 1883. It was destroyed by fire in 1888 and quickly rebuilt. This photograph and that on p.83 of Vol. I, both show long, end-gabled buildings, varying from 1 1/2 to 2 1/2 stories, which appear to be different complexes. The author believes, judging by appearances, that the image here is the rebuilt factory, while the other is the original. (Shrewsbury Historical Society.)

It must have been quitting time at the Hazard plant when this *c.* 1890 photograph was taken. The neatly uniformed workers convey an impression of sanitary conditions. (Shrewsbury Historical Society.)

This Hazard label is affixed to a ketchup bottle and is in remarkably fine condition. It depicts the importance of "Shrewsbury" as a brand name and of the Hazard company's pride in their factory. There are not many factories on labels today. One wonders if the drawing is stylized, as a 3 1/2-story building in 19th century-Shrewsbury does not seem too likely. Their "depot" was a warehouse, in the heart of New York City's wholesale grocery district. (John Rhody.)

53

A newly discovered early photograph of the Hazard Sycamore Avenue house (not available for publication) revealed a Greek Revival-style origin. This c. 1900s photograph, apparently from the rear, presents a large cube with Hazard-added towers behind, making one wonder if it shows the original house. The shadows and ivy contribute to the usual difficulty of researching a house that is no longer standing. This one, deteriorated from long-term vacancy, was demolished in 1937. (Collection Shrewsbury Historical Society.)

James Curley's bachelorhood, as well as his body, came tumbling down in a construction accident. He planned a trip to Florida to convalesce, hoping to take with him his fiancee of 13 years, Emily Sagurton, who was a nurse. Mores of the times forbade it, finally sending them to the altar. At left is best man Robert Sagurton, later a borough building inspector, and at right, maid of honor Katherine Curley. The four are seen at Shadowbrook after the January 1941 wedding.

James A. Curley built his own home, designed by Louis Farmer, with a colonial influence at 245 Sycamore Avenue in 1959. It was built on a former Hazard property, as was much of the Curley homes development. The home was built over a steel beam in the foundation, making its construction distinct.

A good time was had by all at a John Curley birthday party in the early 1960s. Party attendees are from left to right as follows: Giles Whalen, Paul Kolarsick, Deborah Sacco, the birthday boy, Kemberly Kolarsick, Michael Sagurton, Patricia Sagurton, Mark Schissler, Karl Kolarsick, and Nancy Sagurton.

The main block of 130 Sycamore Avenue, built by Louis V. Bell in 1910, is visible on p.96 of Vol. I. Carson C. Peck bought the property in 1916, adding an extension in the rear comprising a 30-by-40-foot Great Room on the first floor. It was designed by Leon Cubberley, is sympathetic to John Hemingway Duncan's original house, and gives the overall structure a "T" plan.

Clara Peck, daughter of Carson, was the Peck best associated with the former Bell property during the family ownership. The resident of Brooklyn was a noted horsewoman and is seen c. 1919 on "Wampum." She was a distinguished horse breeder and officer of the Monmouth County Colt Show Association, often hosting their shows at her Shrewsbury estate, then known as Winganeek Farm. The Pecks sold what had grown to an 80-acre farm in 1932, moving their equine operation to Kentucky. Clara died in New York City in 1953 at age 87.

The south elevation of 468 Sycamore Avenue is seen in a recent photograph, a house likely moved on its plot. The gable end at right probably faced the street at one time. Although the house's lore is traced to the c. 1815 period, physical evidence suggests a c. 1860s structure, perhaps built over an older foundation. Dr. William Van Buren, who lived across the street, once owned the house and conveyed it to his daughter Sara and son-in-law Jules Brugiere. The house is now the residence of Donald and Deborah Burnaford.

An unidentified polo player, perhaps a Hazard, symbolizes the game once played in Shrewsbury.

The Second Empire-style Broadmeadow house at 450 Sycamore Avenue shows little change from a c. 1890s illustration (see p.70, Vol. I) to this 1990s photograph. This southeast perspective shows an extension added to the 1870s main block. The structure is clad with clapboard, built on a brick foundation, and contains a full-length center hall.

Ann Murtha, the Broadmeadow maid for about 50 years, reflects the quiet dignity and countenance of one accustomed to hard work. She was virtually a member of the family, whose closeness was affirmed after her death with a place in the family plot at the Shrewsbury Presbyterian Cemetery. (Shrewsbury Historical Society.)

An unidentified group is seen around the Broadmeadow house c. 1880s. One is tempted to place them on the eastern end of the front porch, suggesting changes in both porch and the bay window on the east elevation. John E. Davis of Red Bank bought the place in 1897. (Shrewsbury Historical Society.)

James Ferdinand Prince, left, and Paul B. Tallman are seen at the gate to the Broadmeadow garden in 1896. (Shrewsbury Historical Society.)

Louisa Dunmore Mott Van Buren,
1821–1892, the wife of
Dr. William Holme Van Buren (Vol. I, p.74),
is pictured with her two daughters, c. 1860s.
On the left is Adelaide who was born 1843,
and married Charles Frederic Meert in 1867.
On the right is Sara who married twice, first
Jules E. Brugiere, who died in 1899, and later
Victor Godfroid Meer (brother of Charles,
despite the difference in the spelling of their
names). Sara wrote a cookbook, *Good Living/ A
Practical Cookery Book for Town and Country*,
published in 1890 by G.A. Putnam and Sons,
New York. (Shrewsbury Historical Society.)

Charles Frederic Meert, born c. 1839,
suffered a failure of an unspecified New
York City business c. 1886. In early
1888, Meert secretly entered his father-
in-law Dr. William Van Buren's former
home at 457 Sycamore Avenue at a
time he had indicated he was returning
to New York and killed himself with
a single gunshot to his chest. Four
days passed before he was discovered.
(Shrewsbury Historical Society.)

The two sons of Charles Frederic and Adelaide Meert are pictured c. 1880s: William at left and Victor. (Shrewsbury Historical Society.)

The house at 459 Sycamore Avenue was formerly a barn, its origin clearly visible in its remodeled state in this 1977 photograph. The Phillipse E.N. Greenes, who lived in a house on the property, made its conversion in the 1940s, but Michael and Dolores Lichtig have made major changes over the past 20 years. A new entrance was built and the doors at right were changed to windows. The shed on the gable end is now an interior room, while a large wing was added at an angle in the rear.

Louis DeCoppet's Thornbrooke, seen c. 1930, was named for his wife, the former Adele Thorn. The 2 1/2-story, Queen Anne-style house was built c. 1880s. (Shrewsbury Historical Society.)

The barn at Thornbrooke is seen looking south when the grounds were open and expansive. (Shrewsbury Historical Society.)

The grounds at Thornbrooke were landscaped, with a variety of specimen trees planted and a special water system installed. Its spillway is seen *c.* 1900. (Shrewsbury Historical Society.)

Many of the Thornbrooke trees were retained as the property was divided, such as the one at left, still on the premises of 451 Sycamore. The house (Vol. I, p.68) was built by Forrest S. Smith, right, a Jersey City lawyer, who is seen here with his daughter Mary Ann shortly before construction.

Sycamore Avenue is seen looking west from in front of Thornbrooke at an unspecified date. (Shrewsbury Historical Society.)

474 Sycamore Avenue was built c. 1890s. Seen in 1964 when it was the Hilton house, the place was earlier owned by J. Wright Brown, a noted stockbroker. The house is little changed, other than by enclosure of the space at left. (The Dorn's Collection.)

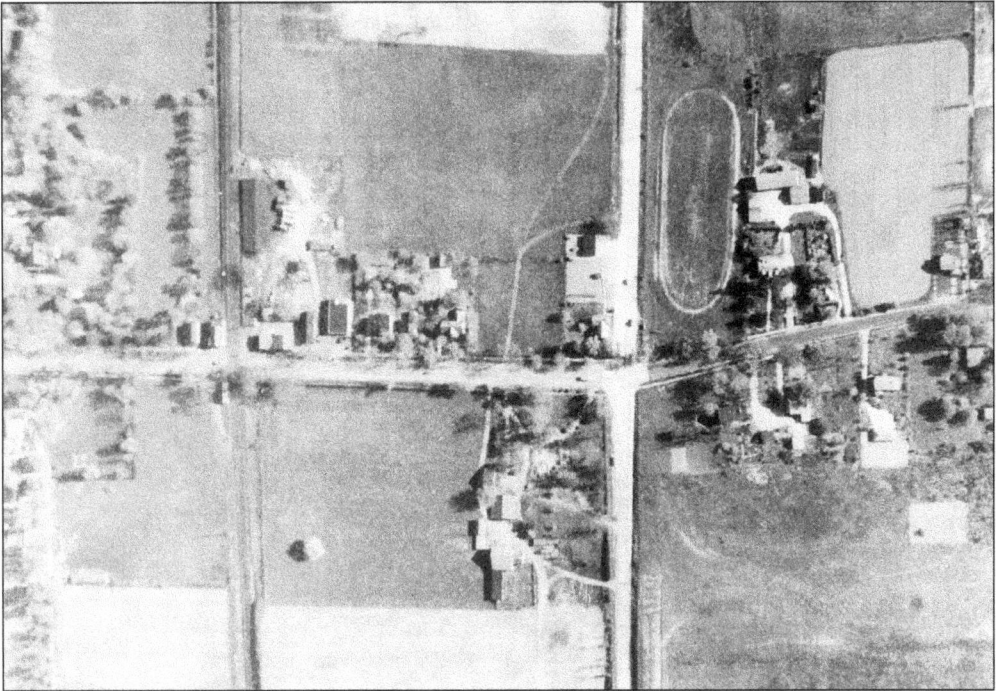

The two vertical bands in this 1938 aerial are the New Jersey Southern Railroad, left, and Shrewsbury Avenue, which is the border between Shrewsbury and Tinton Falls. The Lawes complex is right of the tracks, while two still-standing houses are left of the tracks. Larger Sycamore Avenue houses can be discerned at the left edge amidst the trees. The former E.T. Williams estate on the northeast corner appears intact, the 1936 fire (p.68) notwithstanding.

This view east on Sycamore Avenue, at its juncture with Shrewsbury Avenue, was taken in 1957 from the Tinton Falls side of the border. The former Williams estate is at left on the Shrewsbury side. (The Dorn's Collection.)

The Monmouth County Department of Weights and Measures had demonstration photos taken at Lawes c. 1937, noting their work had increased from fewer than 250 pumps tested in 1916, to 2,800 pumps tested in 1936. Present, from left, were Glenn L. Berry (department supervisor), Patrick Shannon (publisher of Monmouth Pictorial, the source of this photograph), J. Russell Woolley (longtime freeholder from Long Branch), and James S. Parkes (freeholder).

The Lawes plant is seen here in November 1950, with founder Donald Lawes Sr. and his wife Bessie posed in front of a truck. (The Dorn's Collection.)

Donald E. Lawes founded the firm bearing his name in 1926. He is seen celebrating his 75th birthday, receiving a presentation from Velma Dey, at at the office on October 19, 1972. In the middle row, from left to right are: Flora Pierro Bradley, Angie Nelson, Holly Wilson McSorley, and Billy Asbel. Jim Clayton and two unidentified women are in the back row.

Central Jersey Bank and Trust Company was Shrewsbury's first bank, built on the former Williams estate at the northeast corner of Sycamore and Shrewsbury Avenues. The structure is little changed, but banking today has fewer local institutions and more large, distant organizations. This one is now Fleet Bank. Mergers are so frequent that users of multiple banks get statements from strange names and wonder what the bank's name had been when the account was opened. (The Dorn's Collection.)

Edmund T. Williams, a farmer and surveyor, was born 1804 in Colts Neck. He was one of Shrewsbury's leading citizens of the 19th century; Williams built this house at the northeast corner of Sycamore and Shrewsbury Avenues *c.* early 1860s, reportedly one of the first in Shrewsbury with indoor plumbing.

The Williams house incurred considerable fire damage in March 1936. At the time, it was owned by C. Irving Patterson and his sister Mrs. R.B. Wilson and rented to Harry May Jr., who occupied it as the Shrewsbury Farms hotel. A bank is on the site now (p.67).

Three

THE FOUR CORNERS

The *c.* 1825 Lippincott House, now the Shrewsbury Borough Hall, is seen in this *c.* 1940s image, with Sycamore Avenue looking east. The structure is important for its early construction, reflecting significance of Shrewsbury agriculture in the early 19th century, and for its colonial revival alterations, including an addition of about 22 by 40 feet made in 1898 by Edward Kemp. Preserving the building is an important issue as this book goes to press. Regrettably some evaluate the historic structure as square footage of office space rather than as a significant element in what is arguably Monmouth County's most historic acre, Shrewsbury's Four Corners, however, it appears the borough council opted to save the building in a decision just prior to publication.

The second Christ Church edifice, completed in 1774 and shown in original and post-remodeling states in Vol. I, was designed by prominent Philadelphia builder-architect Robert Smith. It was supported by a series of frame trusses running the length of the nave. Trees obscure the 10-foot square tower added in 1874, as depicted in this 1909 photo postcard. (John Rhody.)

Christ Church has long celebrated its history and historical collection. Their Vinegar Bible is one of only about nine copies known to exist today. It is so-named because of a printer's error on the head of the page with the "Parable of the Vineyard," substituting "vinegar" for "vineyard." It was printed by John Basket of Oxford and presented to the church in 1752 by Robert Elliston, Comptroller of His Majesty's Customs at New York.

This ceremonial presentation in 1952 is believed to portray a visiting clergyman from England. (The Dorn's Collection.)

The original Christ Church parish house, designed by Joseph Swannell, has been altered often. It is seen in this 1955 photograph following completion of an expansion designed by D. Wentworth Wright. It stands behind the church. Note its pointed arch windows, similar to those in the church. A variety of church functions and social events are held in the hall, which was also used for services during the 1997–8 restoration. (The Dorn's Collection.)

On a chance inspection of the attic, it was discovered that six of the eight roof trusses had broken in up to five locations each, placing the building in danger of collapse. An extensive restoration project was needed to assure the survival of the building. Interior scaffolding was installed to support structural steel trusses until they were fully assembled. (Christ Church.)

A steel bridge weighing 16 tons was to be installed in the attic. It arrived at the site assembled and had to be disassembled in the yard so each section could be carried in. Each piece could be moved by two men. (Christ Church.)

This photograph shows steel being lowered for the steeple repair, through the steeple's upper section. Steel for the bridge truss entered the building through holes made in the east and west gables. (Christ Church.)

This steel bridge was built to support the building, following a concept by Philadelphia structural engineers Keast & Hood. It was developed at Independence Hall in the 1950s and has been used since in a number of historic structures following systemic failure of roof truss systems. This view in the attic looking east shows one side assembled. The new bridge, supporting two-thirds of the weight of the building, supplements the old truss, which is still framing the ceiling and roof. It was designed so that no part of the original truss had to be cut or removed. (Christ Church.)

Restoration carpenter Ira B. Matthews of Farmingdale is seen at an early shingle-makers bench working 36-inch shingles with a draw shave. The Allen House is in the background. His son, Ira III, is making a replica of the east gable ventilation window removed in 1874. (Christ Church.)

The sharp curvature of the Christ Church dome required shingles to be steamed for bending prior to installation to preclude later lifting. The two Matthews are seen engaged in this process in their Farmingdale yard. (Christ Church.)

74

The support system restoration was also occasion to make repairs to the steeple. This photograph depicts its new steel support. The entire project, one of the most technologically complicated and comprehensive ever, was under the direction of project architect Margaret Westfield, principal of Westfield Architects & Preservation Consultants in Haddon Heights, New Jersey. (Christ Church.)

The foundation was repointed in the 1769 style and new sections of white oak sills were installed; they were made of trees from Monmouth County, as were the originals. The initials and date, believed to be SCM—1769, were found on a stone. They are thought to represent Samuel Cooke—missionary, the rector at time of the original construction. (Christ Church.)

A commemorative program celebrated the newly restored building on April 26, 1998. The larger light fixture is a 1760s English cut crystal chandelier acquired as a memorial to the Reverend James LeSage. The truss failure was originally discovered on a trip to the attic to plan the chandelier's installation. (Christ Church.)

The organ, made by J.H. and C.S. Odell of New York, was first used on December 25, 1879 and is believed to be the oldest remaining intact church instrument in central New Jersey. It was dismantled and removed during restoration and reinstalled by A. David Moore of North Pomfret, Vermont. (Christ Church.)

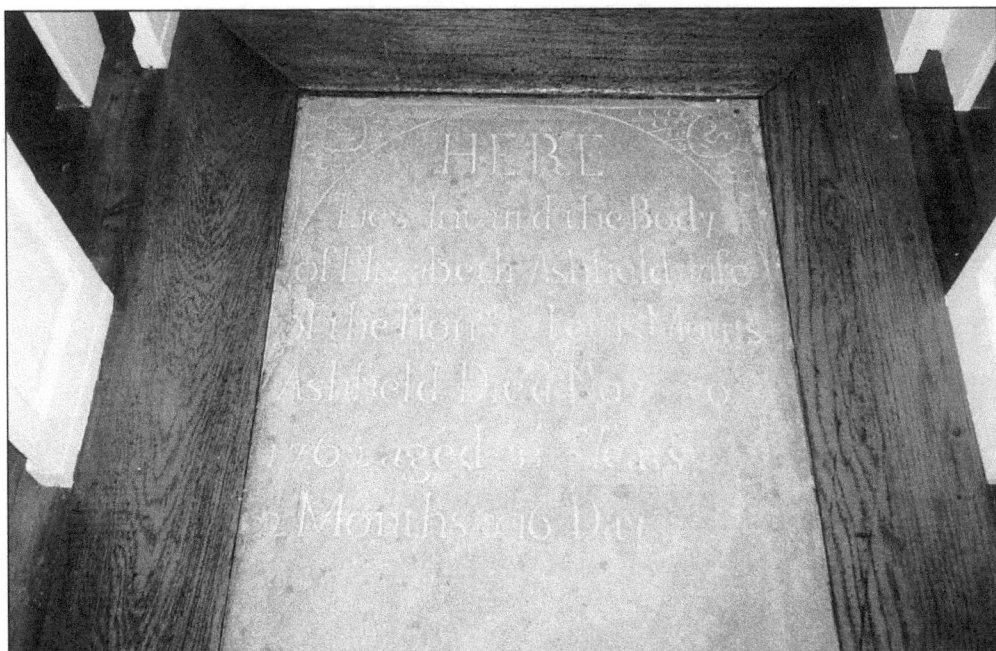

The present Christ Church was built over a portion of their early graveyard. Three tombstones set in the floor of the present building recall internments there. (Christ Church.)

The Edward C. Hazard monument appears near the northwest corner of the Christ Church graveyard. The *Monmouth Democrat* indicated in 1905, when reporting of its installation, that the stone was the work of sculptor Daniel Chester French and bore a fine resemblance to Hazard. It does. Compare this recent photograph with the portrait on p.84 of Vol. I.

This 1950s aerial overlooks the four corners from the southeast. The Presbyterian church is in the center of the image, while its Blair Hall and manse are in the foreground. Christ Church is at left, the view from the rear depicting its 25-foot extension containing a chancel recess, sacristy, and choir robing area. Each of the churches has a cemetery, the two virtually appearing as a single burying ground when viewed from above. The Allen House (p.80) is seen on the west side of Broad, catty-cornered from Christ Church, but the borough hall is out of view. The Quaker Meeting House is on the north side of Sycamore Avenue, opposite the Christ Church parish house (p.71). The Benjamin White house is adjacent to it (p.47). (The Dorn's Collection.)

A group of youths, some with bicycles, are seen in a c. 1910 photo postcard outside the Allen House, suggest its long tradition as a key local meeting place. The house, built perhaps in the second quarter of the 18th century, was a tavern, the home of a physician, and a store in its long history. The store extension at right was built c. 1814. (Shrewsbury Historical Society.)

The Allen House was extensively damaged by fire on April 17, 1914. Abram Holmes Borden's store was destroyed. An earlier post-fire picture on p.29 of Vol. I depicts a still-standing east wing, while this one shows demolition in an advanced state. Borden built a new store across the street adjacent to the Quaker burying ground, which he ran until his death in 1923.

The Allen House later housed an antique shop, which built an extension for displays where the Borden store had been. Its large window showed wares to the heavy traffic at the town's key intersection. Access was by a side door and not through the main building. Note the aptly named occupant in this 1947 image, "The Old House." (The Dorn's Collection.)

Scouts from Shrewsbury Junior Troop No. 352 are seen marching in the Shrewsbury Bicentennial parade passing the Allen House. The parade on May 22, 1976 ended at the nearby borough hall grounds, the site of the Shrewsbury Four Corners Fair held that same day.

The Monmouth Chapter of the Daughters of the American Revolution placed this marker on one of the old sycamore trees in the summer of 1935. The marker has been in storage since the tree was taken down.

The Shrewsbury Town Chapter of the Daughters of the American Revolution is seen with their marker on a sycamore in 1935. Francis Borden is at left, and David Wood is the boy to the right under the flags.

The Monmouth Chapter of the Daughters of the American Revolution met in the Shrewsbury Presbyterian Church on March 26, 1953 to honor three high school seniors who served as their good citizen pilgrims at the state DAR conference. They are from left to right as follows: (seated) Mrs. Raymond Armstrong (state DAR chairperson of good citizens), Mrs. Jacob B. Rue Jr. (chapter regent), and Mrs. Neil G. Clifton (chapter good citizen chairman); (standing) Patricia Mary Dobrowsky (Rumson High School), Jeanne Marie Walker (Red Bank High School), and Carol Mary Lefever (Middletown Township High School). (The Dorn's Collection.)

The Presbyterian Church at Shrewsbury, founded 1732, chartered in 1750, dedicated this Greek Revival edifice on September 29, 1822. A comparison of this c. 1950s photograph with a c. 1900 photo (p.18, Vol. I) shows little change except the removal of a chimney. (The Dorn's Collection.)

The Presbyterian Church held a commemorative service on February 21, 1950 to mark the 200th anniversary of their charter. From left to right are as follows: unidentified, Theodore Parsons, unidentified, Gustav Bottner, and Harold Nevius. (The Dorn's Collection.)

The Reverend David Muyskens, seen in 1978, was a long-term pastor of the Shrewsbury Presbyterian Church.

The Presbyterian church house and manse (p.49) are on Sycamore Avenue, east of the church. The house, named Blair Hall, was originally a two-story building with a 400-seat auditorium set on the rear of its lot and built in 1957. This photograph dates from that period. (The Dorn's Collection.)

A fire, starting in the rear of the building and spreading along the roof, gutted Blair Hall on February 25, 1974, leaving only its walls standing and destroying church records, some of which dated to the late 18th century. Firefighters were hampered by inadequate water pressure. A new one-story Blair Hall was completed in 1977.

Perhaps Shrewsbury's second most curious building was the police kiosk, which stood at the center of Sycamore Avenue, along the east side of Broad Street. It contained a control switch for the traffic light. Otto Herden, born c. 1890, was Shrewsbury's one-man police force and chief. He had a reputation for aggressive enforcement of traffic laws, which was once an important source of local revenue. A quick change of the light, without a long amber pause, made unwary motorists fair game for the chief, seen in a c. 1930 photograph.

Chief Otto Herden is seen in a view looking north on the east side of Broad at Sycamore Avenue. The former house, now an office, at 848 Broad is in the background. Judge Wainwright, the local magistrate was regarded as a virtual co-conspirator in Herden's zealous enforcement of speeding regulations, which received considerable notoriety even outside Monmouth County.

The woman is unidentified, but the occasion of taking her photograph provides a second glimpse of the kiosk. The 1934 image also shows the Quaker Meeting House. The kiosk was removed c. 1942 when Shrewsbury's World War II Honor Roll was erected.

This 1952 aerial looking northwest towards the four corners shows the Presbyterian church, center, prior to the construction of Blair Hall. Christ Church is at left. Notice how their cemeteries appear to be one. The Allen House, above Christ Church, was then painted white and possessed its original dormers (removed in restoration) and show-window extension on the east (p.81). The Presbyterian tower effectively separates the Quaker Meeting House and the Benjamin White house (p.47). Broad Street, the diagonal at top, was sparsely developed. (The Dorn's Collection.)

The Vol. I, p.21 image of the Council Pine shows a much-trimmed tree missing many branches on its north side; it had been on a gradual decline before its c. 1924 removal. This 1896 photograph shows a healthier pine at the center of Sycamore Avenue, east of Broad. The tree is believed to have been planted c. 1835 by Peter Hadden and was once a general meeting place for political orations. Its significance to Shrewsbury tradition is reflected by its presence on the borough seal (p. 92).

Councilwoman Dorothy E. Blair (later Manson) of the council's decorating committee, displays an early valance being reinstalled at the then new borough hall (p.69) before an open house. At left is Frederick J. Mancuso, chair of the renovation committee, and Louis Longo, superintendent of public works. They could not have imagined how much restoration would be needed 20 years later. Dorothy Manson was very concerned about preserving Shrewsbury's heritage. One hopes memory of her accomplishments will inspire wavering voices in current preservation issues, notably borough hall.

The Shrewsbury Historical Society Museum and Research Center (Vol. I, p.81) rose from the ashes of the December 12, 1976 fire that destroyed the carriage house attached to the borough hall property. A senior citizen's or similar center could not be built with available funds, insurance proceeds, and a $30,000 grant. Rather than have the grant declined, the Society obtained authority to use it as the core of financing a museum, and raised funds needed to complete the project. The Society occupies the building behind the borough hall that opened in 1982.

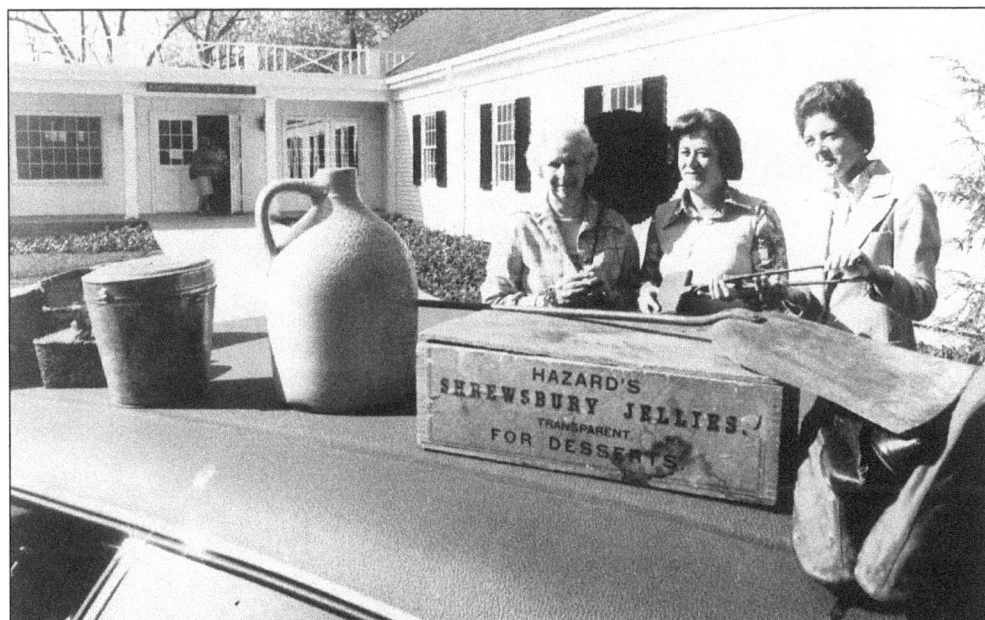

A Shrewsbury Historical Society committee displayed objects that were being organized for their exhibit during the borough's Bicentennial Week celebration in May 1976. Standing outside the Presbyterian church parish house are, from left, Society president J. Louise Jost, Pat Standley, and Mrs. Richard Lackman. Hazard used "Shrewsbury" as a brand name for a variety of products packaged elsewhere for his New York City-based national grocery wholesaling business.

The former post office is seen during its occupancy as the borough hall-police headquarters, with a gathering of seven activists in the 1960 Community Appeal drive. From left to right they are as follows: George Dale (the organization's chairperson), Robert M. Rooke (a director), and Mrs. J. Reid Harrison (corresponding secretary). To the right of the "thermometer," then registering only $2,800 of the $15,000 goal, is Mayor Frederic Messina, Mrs. Wendell L. Rehm, and Mrs. Joseph A Seuffert (both workers), and Charles A. Johnston (publicity chairperson). (The Dorn's Collection.)

Dorothy Blair Manson, seen at her desk in 1979, is in a photograph that reflects the warmth that won her the love of a generation of Shrewsburyites. She is sitting under an image of an eagle, the bird that became her personal totem. Dorothy was appointed to the borough council in 1973 and elected later that year, and again in 1974, and 1977. She was elected mayor in November 1978 and fulfilled a goal to serve 12 years in that office. Dorothy had an untimely death in 1995. (See also: Vol. I, p. 110 and p. 127.)

Shrewsbury (pronounced "shrose-berry") England and Shrewsbury, New Jersey have long enjoyed a sister-town relationship, one that was intensified during WW II as the American town responded to the war-time need of its British counterpart. Mayor Dorothy Blair Manson is seen hosting a tea for Shrewsbury, England visitors in August 1979.

Shrewsbury, New Jersey appears to send a proportionately high number of visitors to Shrewsbury, England in Shropshire. The Lion Hotel pictured on Wyle Cop, c. 1940s, dates from the 16th century. That old street contains a house in which Henry Tudor, soon to be Henry VII, stayed in 1485 before the decisive Battle of Bosworth. The town is best known, however, for Palin's Shrewsbury cakes. (See also: Vol. I, p.128.)

The borough seal of Shrewsbury was adopted in 1944 from a drawing by noted equestrian artist George Ford Morris based on a design by Mrs. Bruce Campbell. Members of the Shrewsbury Historical Society made a needlepoint example in blue and white wool, a two-year project. It was presented to the borough in June 1977 and hangs in the council chambers. Admiring the work that month are from left to right: Dorothy B. Manson, then council president, Mayor Joseph F. Dennis, and J. Louise Jost, president of the Shrewsbury Historical Society.

A Bicentennial flag donated by Shrewsbury State Bank was presented to Mayor Joseph F. Dennis, left, on May 11, 1976. Also at the presentation are, from left to right as follows: Reverend Edward M. Story (rector of Christ Church, also holding the flag), Dorothy B. Manson (borough council president), and Gerald F. Murphy (chairperson of the borough's Bicentennial committee).

92

Four

SCHOOLS

This 1959 aerial illustrates the growth of the Broad Street Shrewsbury Borough School. The 1909 building is the hipped roof structure at left, while the 1935 expansion adjoins it, adjacent on the street. A small expansion on the south side of the old school, completed in 1951, was inadequate when finished. The 1953 one-story addition facing the semi-circular drive is now effectively the main section. A 1958 addition extending to the south, named the Fern Ross Auditorium, is at right. (The Dorn's Collection.)

The 1953 addition, a separate structure later connected to the old building, consisted of ten classrooms, two offices, a stockroom, janitor's closet, and lavatories. This photograph was taken on August 11, 1953 as construction neared completion. (The Dorn's Collection.)

This sign was priced per letter, so one presumes the "boro" spelling was an economy measure. The 1953 addition was called the "middle" building, but in visual and practical terms, it now appears to be the main building. This north facade faces Obre Place. (Photograph by Scott Longfield.)

A vigorous preservation campaign was fought to save the 1909 school. The expected arguments over cost and adaptability of the space were aired before the decision was made to take down the old section. This demolition scene is dated August 25, 1994. (Photograph by Scott Longfield.)

The 1909 school faced Broad and long had an impact as one of the street's major buildings. The 1996 school addition has a severe presence on Broad, likely because architects Thomas Associates, of Ithaca, New York, designed the new building to face Obre Place. The new section is compatible with existing structures, as indicated in this recent photograph. Thus, for practical purposes, the school is no longer a Broad Street building, the presence of a substantial brick wall notwithstanding.

The student body of the old Shrewsbury Borough School was a sizable group. One expects their picture post-dates the 1899 addition of a second room and the hiring of an additional teacher—two are visible in the back. The subjects are unidentified, but "big hair" in the rear used her head to get attention. (Shrewsbury Historical Society.)

Fixed expressions were common a century ago, but this Shrewsbury Borough School group conveys many blank faces. Neither the scene nor subjects are identified in this c. 1890s photograph. (Shrewsbury Historical Society.)

The 1957 eighth graders are seen in front of the Shrewsbury Borough School. The author was in the eighth grade that year. Seeing the mature, smart images of the Shrewsbury students reminded him that many of his contemporaries at PS 24 in Jersey City also cast mature, smart images. (The Dorn's Collection.)

The May 1959 crossing guards are posed for a picture for *The Ivy*, the school yearbook. "Tinker" Dorn is in the back row, second from the right. Their belts and purpose are reminders that Shrewsbury was friendlier to pedestrian traffic before the Broad Street widening, undertaken in the early 1960s. (The Dorn's Collection.)

The photograph is not identified, but the height of the room and the attire suggest the locale is the 1909 school and the time, not long after its completion. Third, Fourth, and Fifth grades are joined here. It is another sign of advancing age, if you can remember when clasped hands on the desk was a regular school position.

This c. 1918 class has two identified students, resulting from their daughter preserving the picture. Emily Sagurton is second from the right in the front row, while her future husband, James A. Curley is fifth from the left in the center.

Painting a map of New Jersey on the school grounds was a 1965 project of the Jerseyana Club. The image seems dated as young artists today would likely be pictured with spray cans rather than brushes. They are, from left to right as follows: Dennis Halsey, Kathy McGuiness, Nancy Koenig, Sandy Savtangelo, and Doug Keiper. (The Dorn's Collection.)

Marie Hamm was born, c. 1905, and raised in Shrewsbury, remaining here after her education as a teacher. She combined effectiveness as an instructor, care, and interest in the individual with a warmth of personality to become one of the borough's best-loved teachers. She lived on Broad Street near the school, which is pictured at right in 1952, and she died in 1995.

Students were clad in ancient garb for the school's Tercentenary pageant in 1964. As is so often the case, he who saves the picture gets his name in the book. John Curley is in the second row, third from the left.

Kenneth C. Pampel taught for 20 years with a spirit and love of music that touched students and staff. He led a local band, the Bokenjo Trio, using his talent for charitable benefactions. Kenn in 1978 was with school band trumpeters Sean Winkel, left, and Scott Patton when his group, having newly recorded an album, was giving a benefit concert to fund school instrument purchases. Pampel died at age 49 in 1997. Fund-raising for a sculptural memorial is underway as this book goes to press in 1998.

Five

PEOPLE, PLACES, AND EVENTS

Dr. Ernest Fahnestock's Shadowbrook, once Shrewsbury's finest country estate, later became the area's finest place of public accommodation. The garden has long appealed to photographers, notably for wedding groups and often with the pergola as a background. The St. Francis Junior League posed there in May 1959, reflecting fashion of the times, including hats and even a fur in late spring. (The Dorn's Collection.)

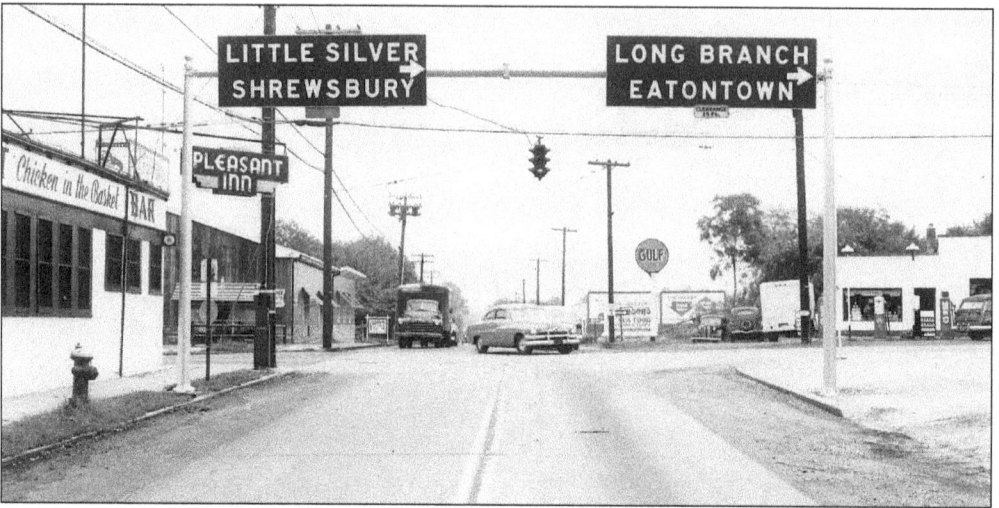

The 1954 opening of the Garden State Parkway increased traffic on Broad Street as motorists traveling east on Newman Springs Road from Exit 109 emptied onto that major state highway thoroughfare. New signs at Newman Springs Road and Shrewsbury Avenue, seen in a September 1954 photograph, were intended to direct traffic along the latter street. The routing could have been misleading to some, as parts of Shrewsbury and Little Silver are more easily accessed by continuing on Newman Springs Road. (The Dorn's Collection.)

This 1960 aerial looks southeast over Newman Springs Road, just east of Shrewsbury Avenue. The long since disappeared house at left, and the rare one still standing on that stem, remind us that the thoroughfare was once residential. The automotive building in the foreground still stands at Nos. 193–5. However, the A&P at center, which is said to have had its business marred by poor visibility from the street, was destroyed by fire in 1978. (The Dorn's Collection.)

James Acerra and Anthony Mazzacco, who opened the Red Bank Recreation Hall containing eight bowling alleys c. 1929, expanded to include an additional eight lanes in 1939. Architect Godfrey M. Ricci of Red Bank gave the building a Moderne appearance as seen in this 1940s photograph. It still stands at the southwest corner of Newman Springs Road and Laurel Street, but bricking-in the windows, changing the entrance, and painting the steel band have marred the appearance, making it look like a warehouse.

The new Matthews Bros. showroom for Jaguars and English-built Fords at the southwest corner of Newman Springs Road and Henry Street is seen in a dramatic night photograph taken on its July 24, 1953 opening. Philip, Richard, and Robert comprised the firm, which had a Hudson agency in Long Branch and sold Willys cars on Newman Springs Road. The building has lost its early character by expansion. The slanted-glass front became popular and imitated after Bernard Kellenyi developed the design in the late 1940s at a nearby Red Bank showroom. (The Dorn's Collection.)

Automobile dealers have traditionally clustered in strips. Once near the center of towns, they have relocated as space needs increased and traffic patterns changed. Red Bank has moved from their initial Monmouth Street-Maple Avenue location to Newman Springs Road, and then, beginning in the 1960s, to Shrewsbury Avenue on the Shrewsbury-Tinton Falls border when the latter town was known as New Shrewsbury. Bud Metcalf's Volkswagen agency at 702, seen in a 1965 aerial, was one of the first there. The business uses a Shrewsbury address in its telephone listing, contributing to imprecise familiarity of place names. The house on the Shrewsbury side is the site of an office. (The Dorn's Collection.)

The old Volkswagen Beetle, long-revered as inexpensive, reliable transportation, was to many in its time, far more. It was often regarded as reflective of a lifestyle and/or a political statement. This volume's 1998 publication is the year of the retro Volkswagen Beetle, which at first glance to the author, seems to suggest that one cannot go home again. (The Dorn's Collection.)

A row of old-style refrigerated Good Humor trucks lined-up at 585 Shrewsbury Avenue, seen here in a 1958 image, should stir memories to any who sought them in the street. After all, the sensory experience was not only the taste of ice cream, but also the sound of the bells, the click of the doors, and the sight of escaping frosty air once the door opened, perhaps for an exciting flavor of the month. One knows these vehicles have reached classic Americana stature as the nostalgia market has produced pricey miniature models. (The Dorn's Collection.)

The Bell Telephone station at 575 Shrewsbury Avenue was typical of the commercial development of the street in the 1960s. It housed repair trucks, as well as an office and is still a facility of Bell Atlantic. (The Dorn's Collection.)

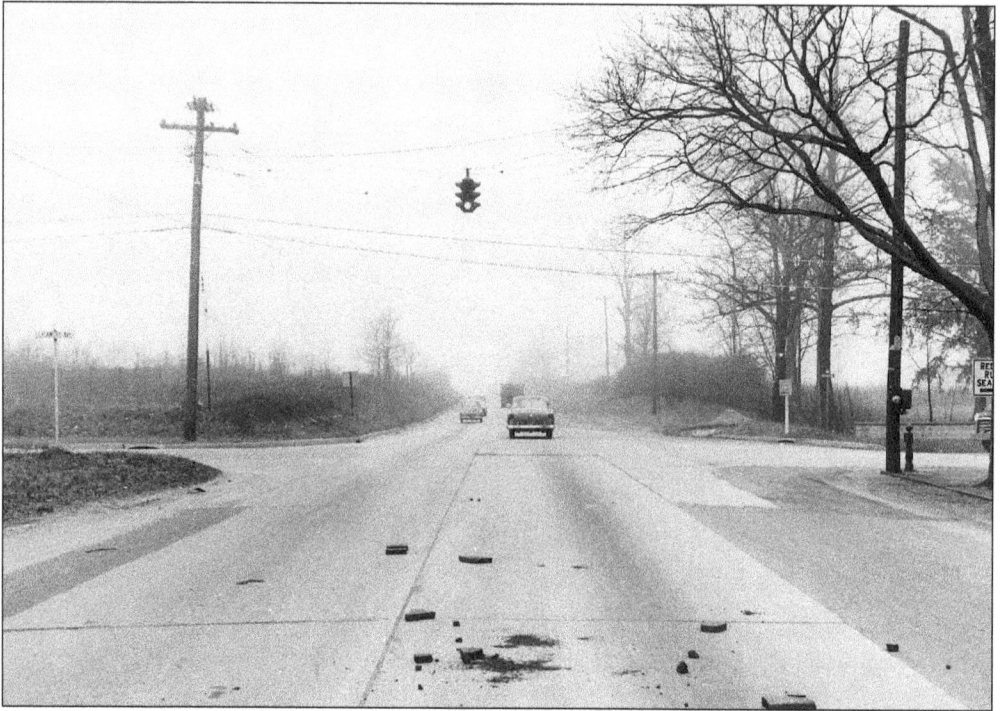

Shrewsbury and Sycamore Avenues in 1957, seen looking north on Sycamore, appeared to be country back roads, this image no longer recognizable following intensive development. The street is Shrewsbury's border with Tinton Falls, visible on the left (west). The Williams estate (see p. 68) was at right. The road today is five lanes at the corner. (The Dorn's Collection.)

The same intersection at top is seen looking south and is also visible in the aerial on p. 65. That photograph depicts a farm with a sizable oval track on the site at the right background, now the location of the Jerral Office Center. A bank was built on the rear of the southeast corner lot, seen on p. 67. A variety of commercial occupancies line both the Shrewsbury (left) and Tinton Falls sides of Shrewsbury Avenue. (The Dorn's Collection.)

The second Shrewsbury station of the Raritan and Delaware Bay Railroad, later the New Jersey Southern and Central Railroad of New Jersey, is viewed looking at its southeast corner c. 1900. It appears to be a beehive of activity, compared with its emptied state on p.122 of Vol. I, but this station transported more produce than people. The station, located near the north side of Sycamore Avenue, was destroyed by fire c. 1950. (Shrewsbury Historical Society.)

The December 19, 1978 accident on the Sycamore Avenue crossing of the Central Railroad's Southern Division did not have the disastrous result of the 1928 White Road accident (Vol. I, p.122), but when the Carbone Trucking tractor-trailer struck a Conrail freight train, it blocked the roadway for 45 minutes. The line is still in use, although one can pass it for years without seeing a train.

The car barns of the Atlantic Highlands Red Bank and Long Branch Electric Railway Company were located on the east side of Shrewsbury Avenue, north of the juncture of the New Jersey Southern Railroad. They housed 20 trolleys and were built in 1896. (Joseph Eid.)

The Shrewsbury trolley car barns were destroyed by an incendiary fire in the early morning of May 24, 1899. Night watchman Peter Morrell discovered flames in an oil-soaked car around 3 a.m. and then flames in another car at the opposite end. Power was off for the night, so he was unable to move any cars to safety. In addition, a gun-wielding thug emerged to prevent efforts to save the place. One suspects the pictured trolleys are replacements stored on the tracks amidst fire-weakened walls, some of which were reported as liable to collapse. (Joseph Eid.)

Laurel Street is seen looking east in the 1930s.

A western view of Laurel Street, c. 1930s, shows several houses, most of which have been raised to add a second story.

Western Patterson Avenue in 1956 still reflected a rural character. The side street is Spruce Drive, while the buildings are Sol Rodack's farm. Chicken coops are at left. New houses line the street today. (The Dorn's Collection.)

Patterson Avenue was an unprotected grade crossing on the Southern Division of the Central Railroad in 1956. The view is east; the house at right is 140 Patterson. (The Dorn's Collection.)

The ball field on the north side of Patterson Avenue is seen from the air in 1954. Allen Street is at left, while 63 and 61 Patterson are the two houses on the north side of the street. (The Dorn's Collection.)

Edd Patterson traveled extensively from his Shrewsbury base during his long career as a magician. His stops included the author's elementary school in Jersey City while he attended in the 1950s. While one would expect any magician to pull a rabbit from a hat, Edd is seen here with Daisy, his daughter Donna's well-trained dog. If Daisy looks familiar, perhaps the reader has seen her in television commercials for AT&T or Buick Park Avenue.

111

Shadowbrook, the finest house ever built in Shrewsbury, merited a chapter in Vol. I. The 1910 summer home of Dr. Ernest and Georgette Fahnestock, designed by New York's Albro and Lindeberg, is seen here in a 1948 image, four years after it opened as a restaurant. The scene is little changed. New balustrades are on the enclosed piazzas, and a canopy has been built over the driveway. (The Dorn's Collection.)

Fahnestock's farm group was built north of his driveway, which became Shadowbrook Drive (to use the one-word version that was adopted after Fahnestock's time). The carriage house-stable in front is also pictured on p. 114, while the bullpen is in the rear of the row. The trees in back line the course of the stream that gave the estate its name. Broad Street is in the lower right corner. (The Dorn's Collection.)

The Shadow Brook rose garden, north of the flower garden between the house and pergola, featured a fine brick fountain designed by Lewis Colt Albro. It was hidden under a protective covering and not "rediscovered" until the last lot in the Shadow Brook development was built-on by Edd Patterson in 1962. Patterson built a California contemporary house which is being greatly enlarged as this book is completed. The fountain's preservation may be observed by comparing the recent image (p.43, Vol. I) with this newly discovered c. 1920 picture.

The gardens of Shadow Brook serve as a fine backdrop for a beauty contest or other gathering, including the 1974 contestants for National Sweepstakes Regatta Queen, which was won by Pamela Jean Behrman of South Belmar, number 13 in the dark swimsuit. To her left is first runner-up, number 15, Regatta Crown Princess Suzanne Franz of Roselle Park. Lynda Orndorff of Eatontown, number six, second from left, was second runner-up.

Ray Stillman bought the Shadowbrook estate in 1942 for a reported $25,000 and subdivided the existing structures and grounds. The farm buildings were remodeled as residences, including the massive U-shaped 1912 carriage house-stable, bought by Tom Howard, the noted radio personality. Howard published this postcard. A quantity fell into anonymous hands, which distributed this one with a hand-written note, "Tom Howard gave me a pack of these to pass to friends out-of-town." (John Rhody.)

Daniel W. Dorn bought the Shadowbrook brooder house in 1943 and remodeled it as a dwelling several years later. The addition of end gables, with one placed on the left, an entry to a garage, shutters, and a fence soon gave the building a residential look. Daughter Kathy remembers best the niches for the chickens, a clear reminder humans were not the first occupants. (The Dorn's Collection.)

114

Susie Lippincott, a niece of Mrs. Edmund T. Allen, struck a pensive, but appealing pose while traveling in Switzerland. (Monmouth County Historical Association.)

Anne Conover Rue, a daughter of Dr. Robert Conover of Red Bank, married Jacob Bergen Rue and long resided in Shrewsbury.

A horse-drawn newspaper wagon in the early 1950s appears to be more of a pose than a delivery system. Bobby Hodgkiss, left, and Bobby Rugg are handing a paper to a customer, likely Annie Gallivan, owner of the pictured and little-changed 34 Thomas Avenue. Hodgkiss, who owned a horse at a time the area was less-developed than today, lived across the street at 35 Thomas. (The Dorn's Collection.)

It appears that two sisters, Emma Sagurton, left, and Jen Beatrice Hounihan, were perhaps worn out from shopping or stayed in the sun too long in 1940. The pose is priceless, although their countenances are less than charming.

Emily Sagurton, born 1907, became a nurse, studying at the Ann May Nursing School. Dr. Ernest Fahnestock wished her to be an operating room nurse for him in New York, but Emily preferred Shrewsbury and an eventual marriage to James Curley. This photograph is her eighth grade graduation. Emily died in 1975.

The charming 18-year-old Emma L. Repphard, not only watched her weight, but recorded in on the rear of this Dehart and Letson photograph of 1902. It was given, "with compliments from the original," when she tipped-in at 148 pounds. Emma worked as a seamstress for Eisner, married John Sagurton, and moved into a cluttered Shadowbrook farmer's house just after redoing her previous residence on Broad Street.

117

The Mill Run office building, 20 Avenue of the Common, probably Shrewsbury's first, appears to be the first tentative intrusion on the landscape. Located behind the Monmouth County Library on the former Straus estate, it was virtually hidden from view. Compare this to recent sizable structures, p.37 for example, and one realizes that commercial construction now makes bold statements on a changed Broad Street. The building is little changed today, except for a round window on the second floor at left.

Frank Arnone's Texaco station is seen on its White Road side in 1961, looking towards Broad Street. This is a replacement of an earlier station facing Broad, the building on the bottom of p. 19. (The Dorn's Collection.)

Silverbrook was begun in the 1930s on the Appleby-Fanshawe estate, but didn't fill-out until the 1950s when many of these houses were built. The view is seen looking west from near number 40, the house at left.

Frank and Fannie Marx are seen *c.* 1930. He was the founder *c.* 1890 of the Shrewsbury meat business, starting as a cattle driver.

James A. Curley is seen in a youthful image.

Curley homes, built east of Broad Street and north of Sycamore Avenue, begun c. 1950, opened Shrewsbury by creating many houses during the post WW II shortage. Built largely on former Hazard property, the development recognized the former farming families by naming streets for them. This aerial is dated October 1955. (The Dorn's Collection.)

The Parker Brothers began their Shrewsbury Gardens development north of Sycamore Avenue in the late 1930s. The area is characterized by generous houses on well-spaced lots.

A group of children posed for their schoolmate Virginia Herden Mohan c. 1950. She recalls them, from left to right, as: (kneeling) Barbara Ingalls, Julie Nevius, Marlene Marx, and unidentified; (standing) Ellen Lethonen, Ina Devries, Ann Jones, Diane Garafalo, unidentified, Gloria Kimball, Sally Duvall, and Charles Marx.

Capt. Jack Edward Mass is seen receiving a citation from the American Legion in June 1953. He served in WW II flying a P47 in Europe as part of the Panzer Dusters squadron that was known for their effective ground strafing action. Jack was a combat pilot with a variety of jets in the Korean War, earning "Ace" status. A test pilot in 1954, he flew an F-104 by 1964, missing an opportunity for a third war when he suffered a stroke. Lt. Col. Mass died in 1968, the day he received notification of a promotion to full colonel. Noted here with thanks to his brother Bucky for the memories. (The Dorn's Collection.)

Bucky Mass recalled his long campaign to make usable for recreation a swampy unbuildable section of Curley homes, soliciting every contractor who passed through Shrewsbury for clean fill. Mass, the newly appointed police chief, asked Mayor White to buy the half that was filled by 1958, then the other half with his promise to fill, a process not finished until 1970. A park was dedicated on May 9, 1959, named the Robert R. Graham Athletic Field, to honor a councilman who served from 1955–57 and died in office of a stroke. Popularly known as Sickels Field, it is located at the north end of Sickels Place. (The Dorn's Collection.)

Raymond "Bucky" Mass, widely known by his nickname, was long Shrewsbury's police chief and served as mayor from 1991 through 1994. Born 1925 in Newark, Bucky moved to Shrewsbury with his family in 1934, as his father became an estate supervisor, the Depression having limited choices as a jeweler. Bucky joined the police in 1952, becoming chief in 1958. Bucky served as president of the Monmouth County and New Jersey Chiefs Associations and of numerous law enforcement bodies. Not a politician, Bucky achieved the mayoralty as an independent, recognizing public office as a route to fulfilling public need.

The New York and Long Branch tracks are the dark diagonal at left. Newman Springs Road, the wide thoroughfare running from it to the lower right corner, forms Shrewsbury's northern border with Red Bank. That town is at lower left. Shadowbrook is east of Broad, in the upper right corner. The course of the stream that gave the estate its name is discernible amidst trees along a dark, curving line. (The Dorn's Collection.)

123

Shrewsbury's northeasterly border is marked by the New York and Long Branch tracks running up and down this *c.* 1960 aerial. The crossing in the center was the site of the 1928 accident pictured on p.122 of Vol. I. Broad Street runs from the railroad to the right edge; the evolution of its northern stem is traced on pp. 10–16. The open field at right is the site of today's shopping center, The Grove. Behind it is the Curley homes development, also seen on p.120. (The Dorn's Collection.)

The Shrewsbury Diner was relocated from the east side of Broad Street near the New York and Long Branch tracks (p.14) to the newly built jug-handle turning lane at the southern tip of Broad by the November 21, 1960 date of this aerial. New stores line the Tinton Falls side of Shrewsbury Avenue, while the Shrewsbury Plaza shopping center had not yet been built on the Shrewsbury side (right). The road widening crowded the roadhouse at lower left, where the Herdens on p. 45 are pictured, a building that today appears dangerously close to the pavement. (The Dorn's Collection.)

Mary Herden Van Brunt Hart and her husband—Van Brunt was killed on D-Day in WWII—
liked to ride horses. She is pictured in the 1940s at lesson time with an unnamed groom.

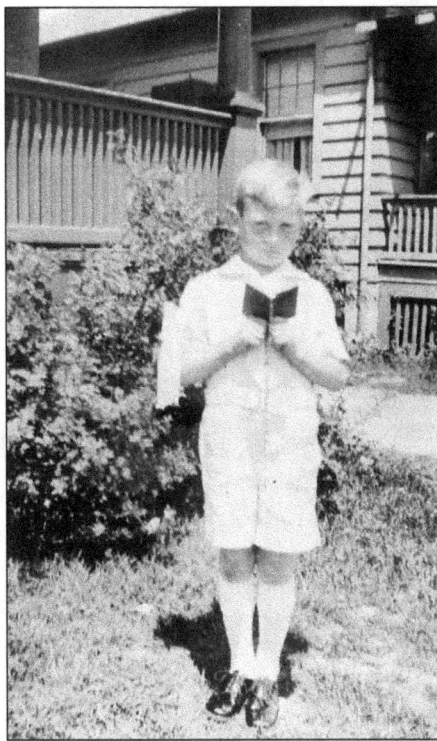

The youthful innocence is captured at first communion of Raymond Herden, uncle of the
lender, Virginia Herden Mohan, who regrettably never matured as he died at age 10 in the
1930s, three years after this image was taken. At left is Mary Brennan Herden, the wife of the
chief on p.86.

125

Kashiro Kodama's Vol. I, p.100 image was a youthful picture taken in Japan; he is seen here *c.* 1920s when he and his wife Mabel Sydney bought the Ethel Kenneth estate to establish "Sunnybank." The Kodamas remodeled a large, old house on the estate, living there for several years as they planned to develop the property, which was mapped for sale by J. Wesley Seaman of Long Branch in 1928. Kodama died in 1941.

The bank of Sunnybank was Parkers Creek and Shrewsbury's border separation from Fort Monmouth, on the south. Kodama's house, built in 1934, is reflected on one of the ponds he built. The 1928 pre-Depression timing was poor. Only one other house was built there prior to WW II, Benjamin Van Vliet's (Vol. I, p.101), but the development filled-out after the war.

In 1929, Frank Quackenbush designed this Tudor Revival house for Morgan C. Knapp. It stood at 21 Buttonwood Drive at the northwest corner of the oval, and is seen here in a 1950s photograph. This image is newer and clearer than the one on p. 109 of Vol. I. It qualifies that books "changed little" comment to the older main block, as a major addition was built on the west side. (The Dorn's Collection.)

A c. 1940s photograph depicting the Frank Quackenbush-designed house at 15 Buttonwood Drive from its southeast corner shows the place prior to the addition of an enclosed entry porch and the maturing of plants (shown on p.110, Vol. I). The early, original buyer of the house, if one existed, has not been revealed, but it is known that developer Harold Nevius sold the house on the western side of the Buttonwood oval in 1955 to George and Dorothy Blair.

Peg bet Jim and won the boat. Knowing that a boat owner's delight at disposing is nearly as great as acquiring, maybe Jim did not feel as if he lost. Actually, the "slogan" reflects the diminutives of the three pictured Curley children, Emily Margaret (now Kaeli), Elizabeth (now Wurst), and James Jr., in an early 1950s image.

Robert Pierce, right, was a laid-back character, who lived in the distant past and had a penchant for telling long tales, recalled Tom Mohan. His wife Virginia added, "Uncle Bob had two horses, Dan and Dolly, plowed fields for farmers well-into the 1950s and went into hay rides as a sideline." "It was typical of the fun we had in the fifties," recalled Kathy Dorn Severini. Author's advice: "Enjoy the ride!"

128

www.ingramcontent.com/pod-product-compliance
Lightning Source LLC
Chambersburg PA
CBHW080907100426
42812CB00007B/2197